MEETING DEATH

MEETING DEATH

Margaret O. Hyde
and
Lawrence E. Hyde

Walker and Company
New York

First published in the United States of America in 1989
by the Walker Publishing Company, Inc.

Published simultaneously in Canada by Thomas Allen & Son
Canada, Limited, Markham, Ontario.

Printed in the United States of America

Library of Congress Cataloging-in-Publication Data

Hyde, Margaret O. (Margaret Oldroyd), 1917–
    Meeting death / Margaret O. Hyde.
        p.   cm.
    Bibliography: p.
    Includes index.
    Summary: Provides information to promote the acceptance of
the concept of death, discussing such aspects as the terminally
ill, suicide, grief and mourning, and the treatment of death in
various cultures.
    ISBN 0-8027-6873-3. ISBN 0-8027-6874-1 (lib. bdg.)
    1. Death—Juvenile literature.   2. Bereavement—Juvenile
literature.   [1. Death.]   I. Hyde, Lawrence E.   II. Title
HQ1073.3.H93   1989
306'.9—dc19   88-27933
                                                            CIP
                                                             AC

10 9 8 7 6 5 4 3 2 1

All of the artwork decorating this book is from *Early New England
Gravestone Rubbings* by Edmund Vincent Gillon, Jr., Dover
Publications, Inc.

Book design by Laurie McBarnette

CONTENTS

Foreword

As modern technology makes it possible to prolong life and mandates changes in the way death is defined, it is imperative that young people talk about death and dying. *Meeting Death* affords an excellent springboard for exploring a subject that needs to be sensibly discussed before one becomes emotionally involved with it.

Meeting Death helps to promote more comfortable acceptance of the terminally ill as people who are living until they die. It suggests ways to deal with grief at the death of a loved one and ways to interact with a suicidal person.

The authors help young people to meet

death in a matter-of-fact and nonmorbid manner through a framework of information that provokes each reader to formulate his or her own concepts about death. When there is acceptance of death as life's most obvious truth, life has more meaning.

—Elizabeth Forsyth, M.D.
Child Psychiatrist

MEETING DEATH

CHAPTER
1

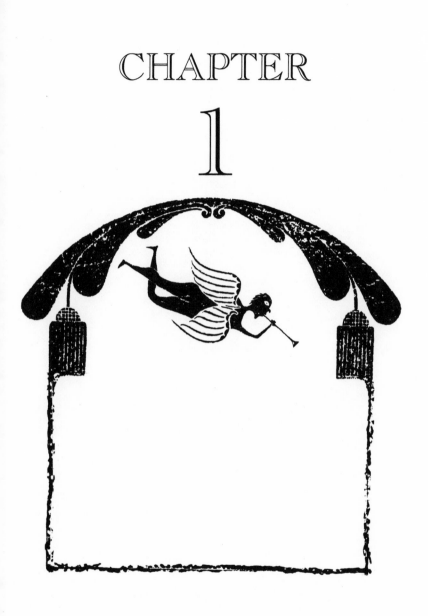

Meeting Death

How do you react to the word death? What comes to mind? Skull and crossbones? Cemeteries that are scary at night? Funeral processions? Devils and angels? Families in mourning? A mystery story? Does the subject make you uncomfortable?

Death education is growing in popularity because it helps to remove the myths and taboos about death and enables people to deal with the subject rationally. Many individuals who are dying are not treated as human beings because people around them suffer from death-related anxieties. Death education helps to promote comfortable and intelligent interaction between the living and the termi-

3

nally ill. Learning about death helps to develop a reverence for life. Those who meet the death of someone close or think about dying consider the fragility of life and tend to rethink their own values and to work for peace. Among other things, the study of death helps people to live decently and die well.

Psychiatrists tell us that we cannot truly imagine our own natural death. In our unconscious, if life has to end, we feel it will be because of something that happens from the outside, such as an automobile accident, or even a murder. This idea is not surprising if your only experience with death is seeing a violent happening on the television news.

In years gone by when more people died at home as part of a family that included several generations, young children were familiar with peaceful death. When Granny's grandmother died, the family washed her body, dressed her in her best clothes, and laid her in a coffin that one of them had made. They surrounded the coffin with flowers, and, whenever her family felt like it, they could wander into the room where she lay and spend some time with her body. In those days many homes had a room called a parlor that

4

was reserved for special occasions like weddings and funerals. No one ever used the room for anything else. After many neighbors and friends had called to say good-bye, this grandmother was buried in the cemetery at the nearby church.

People were more familiar with death in those days, partly because more people died at home, but also because more people died at an early age from diseases that have since been conquered. Many children lost their brothers and sisters, and even their parents, from diseases that now can be cured by modern medicine. Today, many people live to be quite old, then die in a hospital or nursing home. We have little contact with the dying or with those who have died.

Today as children we will probably first meet death in a horror film or in crime dramas on television or in the movies. Death is common in spy stories, Westerns, war stories, and of course, in detective stories. We watch news reports of disasters in which people die. Deaths in the midst of earthquakes, floods, and traffic accidents are familiar sights. But these deaths are not as real to us as the death of a friend, someone in the fam-

5

ily, or even a pet. With the exception of the explosion of the space shuttle, the deaths we see on television are anonymous.

We hear about threats of death by nuclear extinction. Will death come in a flash for everyone on the earth? Such an idea is too horrible to imagine. Perhaps there has been so much talk about nuclear war that the thought of death by nuclear attack does not really mean much to the listeners.

Certainly, we learn about death quite differently from the way people met death generations ago. We are learning how to deal with death in a different way, too. But although death education can help, no one really knows the best way to think about death, for death is a part of life that remains fundamentally unknown.

Who wants to talk about death? Once, the answer was no one, or only the people who are facing death. Today, there are new attitudes about death. There is a trend of accepting death as a part of life and even as the final stage of growth. People are beginning to discuss the subject with children of all ages, having learned that the more they avoid the idea that death is a fact of life, the more they fear it. Many experts believe it is really death that gives life urgency and significance. People who have come near death say that the experience gives life new meaning.

Everyone actually begins to die at birth. In fact, everyone "dies" at least a thousand deaths a day till bodily death puts an end to this dying. The cells that die are replaced by other cells at a rate that supports your growth, and when you stop growing larger, the rate slows. When you grow old, the body cells wear down faster than they grow and repair themselves. Old people actually shrink in height.

Some of the dead cells in your body can be noticed on your head. Your hair is made of dead cells; it grows because of the live cells at the roots. Dandruff and fingernails are other examples of dead cells you can see. When a cast is removed from an arm or leg that has been broken, sheets of dead skin cells are found beneath the cast. Dead skin cells are normally shed so that you do not notice them, but they have no place to go when there is a cast holding them. You probably have not thought much about the cells in your body that die, but they illustrate the point that death is part of your life. As part of you has died since you began to read this sentence.

You probably do not remember much about your first ideas of death. Sometimes, children think about death in strange ways because of something they have heard or seen.

Ben is only five years old. He does not think about death, although he has seen many people die on the television screen. These deaths meant little to him. When his father took him fishing, he watched the preparation of fish for cooking. When the head was cut off the first fish, he remarked that it was really dead. He knew the bugs he squashed with his foot died, but death meant little to him personally until his own cat, Grey, died.

Ben wanted to plant Grey in the ground with the daffodils, so that the cat would come back to life when the daffodils came up in the spring. Ben's parents tried to help him understand that his pet would never be alive again. There was nothing anyone could do to make it purr or curl up in his lap the way it had yesterday. The cat would no longer feel, move, see, eat, or do any of the things that add up to being alive. They explained that all living things had beginnings and endings.

8

Plants and animals are being born, living their lifetimes, and dying all around us. The time for Grey to die had come.

After Grey was buried in the woods behind his house, Ben thought about him often. He liked to imagine the cat living happily on a spaceship that was speeding around the earth. There it would be weightless, and it could jump as high as it wanted to. But Ben wished the cat had not died. He really did not want to talk about its death.

Seven-year-old Gary has met death by watching the news on television. A plane has been hijacked and one of the hostages has been rolled out of the plane onto the ground after being shot. Gary tells his mother that he does not want to die, but he believes that someone will shoot him soon.

Here are some other ideas that young people have expressed when they were asked about dying.

- Eight-year-old girl with cancer: When you die, all the pain goes away and you are happy. No one can stick a needle in you because you will not have a body.

9

- Nine-year-old boy: When I die, I will climb a ladder into the sky. Then the angels will pluck me from the clouds.

- Ten-year-old boy: Dying is like jumping off a diving board and disappearing.

- Eleven-year-old boy: When I die, I will go to heaven and be changed into something new for another life on earth. I hope I have some say in what that will be. I would hate to be a snake.

- Twelve-year-old girl: When someone dies, they are laid in a coffin, and, when the lid is closed the spiders will spin cobwebs around their dead bodies. When they are lowered into the ground, their bodies rot.

- Twelve-year-old girl: When you die, your soul goes to heaven and joins other souls. Sometimes, it comes back to earth and acts like a guardian angel to someone you love.

Some children felt that they would be surrounded by darkness when they died, while others felt that they would be surrounded by light. Most agreed that they would die someday, but there are children who say they hope they will never die. One child said, "Dead is dead. I would rather live."

When is a person really dead and what happens to the body when a person dies? Can a person die more than one death? How can one help to prevent the suicide of a friend? Do you want your body to live if your brain is dead? How do people care for the dead? How can one best deal with the loss of someone close? These are just a few of the questions discussed in this book. From strange ideas about ghosts and spirits arising from dead bodies to attempts at protection from them to thinking about one's own death as a fact of life, the study of death can help to enrich the lives of people of all ages.

Death is usually seen in a negative light, but Dr. Elisabeth Kübler-Ross, in her book *Death: The Final Stage of Growth,* speaks of the study and experience of death as one of the most productive avenues of growth. Certainly, learning about death can help one to cope with the mysteries and fears that surround it and give more meaning to one's own life.

11

CHAPTER
2

Ghosts, Superstitions, and Celebrations

Many dark, supernatural mysteries surround death. In the primitive past, when death was ascribed to supernatural causes, innumerable kinds of magic were used to ward off evil spirits, and some of the rituals have persisted to the present day.

In many cultures, people found the corpse to be unpleasant and frightening, and this aversion is present to some degree today in countries around the world. Part of this feeling may be due to the shock that the living experience after someone dear to them can no longer speak, move, or participate in the everyday world.

The dead body may be a source of fear

15

because people connect it with disembodied spirits, and these feelings may have been present as far back as the time of the caveman. Scientists believe that early peoples may have explained their dreams as visits from spirits of those who had died.

Through the years, it was widely believed that the spirit of a dead person felt excluded from its former existence and wanted to return to life. If the spirit failed to come back, it might try to take others with it to the grave.

When a person died violently, and/or had some unfinished business, the ghost could have a strong motive for wanting to return or get back into the world. People who were murdered, or who had some other reason for vengeance, were often buried at crossroads, partly because of the magic power of the cross, and partly in hope that the ghost of the person might not take the right road to find his enemies.

Ghosts of young people were especially feared, since they were believed to have considerable strength and energy. In some groups, an unmarried person was considered to have unfinished business, but a mock marriage at the funeral would serve to protect the living from the ghost. Ghosts of women who died in childbirth were considered particularly dangerous, for they, too, had unfinished business.

Ghosts are sometimes believed to be spirits who have been given extra rewards or special punishment. In primitive societies, ghosts and other spirits are thought to range over the entire community, while in China and other ancestor-worship civilizations, spirits dwell in shrines that are located in homes or family burial plots. In Thailand, for example, ornate spirit houses occupy a prominent place in the family area. Symbolic contact with the dead may be a daily occurrence, even in current times.

Superstitions about spirits are still common in many places. Often mirrors in a room where the corpse is present are covered to prevent the newly departed spirit from being trapped there. A plate of salt in the room with the dead person is supposed to overcome evil powers that might be lurking. All knots in the room are supposed to be untied to prevent the ghost from being caught in them.

The ringing of a church bell not only calls

people to the funeral, but, according to some believers, it drives away the evil spirit. If a dog or cat jumps over the body of a person who has died, or over the coffin, it must be killed immediately to avert bad luck.

The famous Irish wake grew out of the fear of evil forces from the dead body. Those who keep the corpse company must stay awake, hence the name "wake." Cars in funeral processions put on their headlights, often as a way to keep the funeral procession together, since most drivers, in respect for the mourners, will not interrupt the procession. However, in earlier times, lights were supposed to scare away evil spirits. Cutting into a funeral procession was believed to direct the wrath of the ghost toward the intruder.

The custom of hanging wreaths on the doors of houses where people have died continues in some parts of the United States. It began because people believed the wreath would bind the dead spirit and prevent it from returning.

Mourning veils and somber clothing are still worn to many funerals in respect for the dead and the families of the deceased. This custom is believed to come from attempts to hide one's identity so that the ghost of the person who died would not recognize the mourner and haunt him or her.

Just about everywhere, ghosts are thought to be the spirits of dead people who are endowed with wills of their own and with the ability to move where they wish. Most ghosts were considered evil, especially if they were spirits of people who had died violent or unnatural deaths, or who were improperly buried.

Scientists who have studied customs around the world find many similarities in the efforts to get rid of the ghosts of the dead. Fire is part of many ceremonies. Some are lighted to protect relatives of the dead person from the ghost. Some are lighted so that smoke can be a pathway for the spirit to rise to heaven, thus eliminating the chance of the ghost's wandering around on earth. In some cultures, the hands and feet of the corpse are bound; sticks and thorns are strewn over the pathway to the grave site to prevent the ghost from returning. An extreme measure is practiced by a tribe in Queensland, Australia, where the head is cut off after a person dies. The head is roasted in a fire on the grave and

19

then smashed and left in the hot coals. Mourners believe that the ghost who arises from the grave will miss his head and go groping for it in the fire, where he will be scorched and so be glad to return to the cramped quarters of the grave.

In more sophisticated cultures, ghosts are relegated to stories, although many children are afraid to pass a cemetery after dark, and people of all ages have been frightened by noises in their homes at nighttime. The dead, their ghosts, and the houses they supposedly haunt hold a great deal of fascination, not only for those who believe in ghosts, but also for those who know they do not exist.

Many superstitions about the dead and their ghosts still continue. For example, one must not step on a grave and incur the wrath of the dead. If one does happen to step on a grave, jumping backward over it will appease the ghost.

The laying of wreaths on graves probably comes from the custom of giving gifts to the dead and placing them on the grave to appease the ghost, but, as on doorways, wreaths may be considered a magic circle to bind the ghost and prevent it from returning.

Good ghosts were believed to make their appearance to two young sisters in Hydeville, New York, about 1848. These girls talked to ghosts, or spirits, through raps that were heard in response to their questions. The spirits reached living people through the girls. Not everyone believed in this ghostly form of communication, but those who did banded together to create what is now known as spiritualism. Some people believe that one can converse with the dead through a medium, a person like the Fox sisters, who can communicate with spirits. They still consult individuals who claim they can talk can talk with their dead relatives and friends. Many spiritualists, who conduct "seances," or sessions for summoning spirits, have been shown to have secret devices that make the spirit world appear to be authentic. However, those who believe are often willing to spend large sums of money in their efforts to communicate with the dead.

The ghosts of Halloween are recognized as children in costume, but the celebration continues year after year. Halloween is the eve of All Hallows, or All Saints Day. In some faiths, this is a day devoted to the memory of those who have died and gone to heaven. Even in pre-Christian times it was a day devoted to the memory of the dead. The skulls, crossbones, devils, witches, and ghosts are symbols of death and are part of the Halloween celebration. One appeases the ancestral souls who return from the dead (in the form of costumed children) with candy and small tokens. In ancient times, candy and small tokens were offered on the graves of the dead. This was considered payment for fare over the river Styx, on the way to the underworld. If the soul did not get across the river, it could haunt the survivors on earth.

Skulls and crossbones and entire skeletons are still considered fascinating and are the subject of various forms of art. Mugs in the shape of a skull, mugs made from actual skulls, trophies decorated with symbols of death, lampshades made from human skin, books bound in human skin, shrunken heads, and other mementos that deal with death are popular in celebrations that honor the dead.

In Mexico, the Day of the Dead (All Saints Day) was a time when families prepared the special foods of loved ones who had died.

Women and children took the food to the cemetery at midnight and sat around the graves in candlelight. Marigolds, food, and images of household saints were placed on the grave. After a while, the food was taken back home and eaten. Prayers for the dead were said the next day, and, in the evening a performance of *Don Juan* ended with a dance of skeletons. In parts of Latin America, images of death, such as candy skulls, pottery and paper-mâché figures of skeletons, and numerous masks are still popular at this time of the year.

As death became less frightening and ghosts seemed less likely to rise from the graves, tombstones grew smaller. Heavy stones were no longer needed to hold the corpse and its ghost in the ground, and families were alerted to cheaper ways of marking graves that were still considered respectful. Lawn cemeteries, or memorial parks, came into vogue in many areas, but in some cemeteries gravestones are still a matter of pride.

Groundskeepers in cemeteries complain that tombstones interfere with the operation of large mowing machines, but tombstone makers still encourage decorative markers.

23

There are claims that personalized stones are gaining in popularity. Modern fine-tipped drills have enabled tombstones engravers to depict sketches of houses, boats, and even smiling portraits of individuals. Persons who care deeply about their tombstone often arrange to have it in place while they are still alive in a last effort to celebrate their favorite hobbies or possessions.

Or do they somehow believe that they will take the real house, boat, or golf clubs with them? For, although they admit that they will die, and have made preparations for their death, they, like all humans, have difficulty in believing that life, for them, really will end. For each one, death is a premature event.

CHAPTER

3

What Is "Dead"?

No one really knows exactly what happens when a person dies. Scientists have defined and redefined death, and religious leaders have presented many beliefs about what happens to the spirit. Almost no one argues about defining death as the absence of life from something that has been living, but finding an exact definition for what it means to be alive is difficult. For example, a virus seems to qualify as living when it invades a cell that enables it to reproduce, but without the living cell, a virus is considered nonliving, since it cannot reproduce. Is the virus dead? What about bacteria that have been frozen in Antarctica for thousands of years? In favorable conditions such

bacteria have been revived and have repro-
duced. Would you consider bacteria that have
been frozen for a thousand years among the
living if you did not know that they could
still reproduce?

What about people who arrange to have
their bodies frozen after they die? A small
number of people have had their bodies frozen
as soon as they die with the hope that they
can be thawed at a time when medicine is
more advanced and then cured of the diseases
that killed them. Scientists have little hope
that such persons will be brought back to
life, even if the freezing process begins immediately, but just suppose they could be.
Would you consider them dead while they
were in the frozen state?

Picture the case of John (not his real name),
a member of the Cryonics Society of New
York, who actually had arranged to have his
body frozen upon his death. After he died, at
the age of twenty-four, members of the Cryonic Society began applying ice packs to his
body soon after it was delivered to them from
the hospital morgue, where it had been kept
under refrigeration. An undertaker injected
into John's blood vessels a chemical that

28

might help to protect his cells from the damage caused by freezing. Freezing normally destroys tissue by crystallizing the water in and around cells. Replacing the blood with a variety of antifreeze solutions was an effort to avoid severe damage.

John's body was then cooled for several hours by placing it in a plastic bag filled with ice. Next it was transferred to a Styrofoam-insulated box that was packed with dry ice for the funeral. About a month later, John's body was placed in a long capsule of liquid nitrogen, which must be serviced regularly to keep the nitrogen at the proper temperature.

Suppose, after a hundred or more years, with the help of cloning and gene manipulation, John might be given some additional years to live. Would his body have been dead or just living in cryonic suspension? More than a dozen people are now being stored in nitrogen-cooled capsules at three storage centers in the United States, but, so far, scientists have not even been able to make use of frozen organs for transplant surgery.

There are cases of children who have been revived after being "drowned" in very cold

water. Their conditions were reversible because the cold prevented permanent damage
to their cells. Death comes in stages. Even
though people are clinically dead, changes
may be reversed in some cases. Cold slows the
dying process, but once the body has passed
the stage where the cells in the brain are
deprived of oxygen and have been destroyed,
death is irreversible.

Brain cells in the part of the brain known
as the cerebrum normally begin to die four to
six minutes after they are deprived of oxygen. This part of the brain is the part that is
responsible for conscious and voluntary ac-
tions. It is the part responsible for learning
and memory, problem solving, and the meaningful part of human lives. The lower centers
of the brain can continue to control the invol-
untary functions, such as the circulation of
blood and breathing, even after the cerebrum
is destroyed. A person whose cerebrum has
ceased to function might live in a coma for a
long time. In one case, a man whose cerebral
cortex was completely shattered in an automobile accident lived four years without mov-
ing a single muscle of his body. He felt no
stimulus from within or without. All thought

and feeling were erased at the time of the accident, which occurred when he was sixteen years old. At the age of twenty, he looked like a ten-year-old with a baby face.

If a person falls into a coma when the cerebral cortex is not destroyed, there is a possibility of regained consciousness and a return to normal life. Doctors can determine whether or not there is electrical activity in the cortex of the brain through the use of a machine known as the electroencephalograph. This knowledge has given the medical profession a new way to define death. The absence of electrical activity in the brain is called brain death. However, not everyone is willing to accept this definition of death.

Glen was riding his bike home from school when a drunken driver smashed into him. He was rushed to the hospital, but the doctors could do nothing to repair the damage to his brain. Glen was put on a life support system, which made him continue to breathe and made his heart continue to beat, supplying oxygen to his tissues. At first, his parents refused to believe that there was no hope for Glen to live on his own, but the doctors explained that his brain had been damaged se-

31

verely, and he could not breathe without the machinery to which he was attached.

A social worker discussed with the parents the possibility of using Glen's organs to save the lives of other people who were waiting for transplants. At first, Glen's parents refused, but later they decided that Glen would have wanted this. It would give some meaning to his death if other lives could be saved. In a sense, he would live on in the bodies of the people who received the transplants.

As soon as permission was given, Glen's heart, his lungs, his liver, his kidneys, and the corneas of his eyes were harvested. His body was prepared for burial in such a way that no one would know these organs were missing. There was a viewing, at the request of his parents, and those who wished to say their farewell to the body were able to do so at that time. Glen's parents would never fully recover from the tragedy of their son's death, but they took comfort in knowing that three people would continue to live because of the organs that were given for transplants. In addition to this, a person who had been blind for seven years was able to see again because of the corneal transplants.

Claire has considered signing a donor card, one that gives permission for doctors to use her organs for transplants when she dies. Claire knows that it is unlikely that she will die while she is young enough so that her organs are usable for transplant, but she is among a growing number of young people who realize the value of signing donor cards. When they do so and discuss their wishes with their families, they make it easier for those who must make a decision if a tragedy should occur. Hospital staff are asked to discuss the possibility of organ donation when there is a sudden death of a young person. There are long waiting lists for transplants, and teams of medical workers are prepared to spring into action as soon as they have news of available kidneys, hearts, and other organs.

David would like to sign a donor card, but he worries about the possibility of a transplant team springing into action too soon. "Suppose I am not really dead?" he asks. "Suppose the doctor has a friend who needs a heart, so he takes mine before all hope for me is gone?" He does not know that physicians other than transplant surgeons must confirm that death has occurred. Their conclusion about death must be reaffirmed at a later period before any organs are harvested for transplant.

Today, there is often a fine line in defining life and death. Rudy lies in a hospital bed with a life support system connected to his body through a maze of tubes. His body wastes are excreted without his knowledge and are carried by some of the tubes into plastic sacs. He has been in a coma for six months, but his mother insists that he can hear her when she talks to him. She sits by his bed, day after day, waiting for him to open his eyes. The doctors know that his brain has been damaged, and there is no hope that he will ever recover. His heartbeat and his breathing would have stopped months ago if they had not been continued by artificial means. But, according to his mother, Rudy is alive. According to the doctors, Rudy is brain dead.

Patients with hopelessly damaged brains can be kept alive for indefinite periods of time through the use of respirators. In one case, a patient was kept alive for eight years. Cases have been reported in which autopsies

showed that the brains of patients had lique-
fied before heart and lung machines were
removed. The time of such a death would
remain uncertain.

Suppose you are on duty in a hospital
where a person has died. One of the questions
on the many forms you must fill out asks the
time of death. Sometimes the exact minute is
important, especially when a husband and
wife die at approximately the same time. The
disposition of their estate might depend on
which one dies first. In the case of the person
you are reporting, you have checked heartbeat, blood pressure, and pupils of the eyes.
There was no response. But exactly when did
the man die? The nurse reports one time, and
you finish your examination at another. But
his heartbeat stopped about twenty minutes
ago, and you know that he cannot be revived.
Knowing what happens in the various stages
of death, do you find it easy to pinpoint the
time?

When is dead, dead?

This is a question that has been answered
in different ways as definitions of death have
changed. For many years, a doctor would
decide that a person was dead when there

was no evidence of a heartbeat. When a mirror held in front of the nose showed no presence of moisture from the exhaled breath, it was determined that breathing had stopped. Another sign of death included, and still includes, dilated pupils that do not respond to light. When a person is dead, there is no reaction, even when a lighted match is held in front of the pupil. The mouth may be open and motionless, and the skin turns pale and cold. After about fifteen minutes without oxygen, the brain dies completely and the other systems of the body, which no longer receive messages to function, shut down. Some parts of the body will continue to work for a period of time. For example, kidneys work for another thirty minutes to two hours.

The muscle cells retain enough energy to stay relaxed for about two hours, but when they are no longer able to hold their normal stretched position, they contract, and the body stiffens. The body is now in the well-known state of rigor mortis, a condition that lasts for about thirty hours. Then the muscle cells soften, but they do not return to their original condition. The cells are dead.

During the state known as rigor mortis,

the body is already beginning to decompose. A wide variety of organisms are attacking the tissues, and when the hemoglobin is released from the red blood cells, one can note discoloration of surface tissues. Gases bloat the body, eyes bulge, and the swollen tongue protrudes. The process of decomposition continues until only the teeth, skull, and bones—the skeleton—remains.

CHAPTER

4

Death and the Children

Ideas on talking to children about death have varied a great deal through the years. While early people accepted death as a natural part of life, Puritans used it as a threat and a means of discipline. If you lived in Puritan times, your Sunday mornings might have been spent listening to a minister preaching about the horrors of hell. The youngest most vulnerable members of the congregation were the targets of preachers who felt obligated to instill the fear of dying into them. The Puritans lived in fear of hell, since their doctrine taught that no one could be sure whether he or she was among the small group God had chosen to go to heaven. The rest were slated for damnation, and this included the children who were not among the chosen. There is some mystery as to why this knowledge encouraged good behavior.

James Janeway's famous book *A Token for Children* was written to remind children of the eighteenth century about the ever-nearness of death and its consequences. Puritan children learned alphabet rhymes from the *New England Primer* that included many mentions of death. For example, "G—As runs the Glass/Man's life doth pass." "T—TIME cuts down all/Both great and small." "X—XERXES the great did die/And so must you and I." "Y—Youth forward slips/Death soonest nips."

Cotton Mather, a famous Puritan preacher, advised, "Go into Burying Place, CHILDREN; you will there see GRAVES as short as your selves. Yea, you may be at PLAY one Hour; DEAD, DEAD the next" . . .

Children of the nineteenth-century Romantic and Victorian eras were also instructed to think about death, but, in contrast to the children of the Puritan era, they were to picture death as a transformation similar to the releasing of a butterfly from a cocoon. For

Christian children, reunion with loved ones in heaven was stressed, along with the sweet glory of salvation.

As recently as fifty years ago, many children were taught to say the following prayer each night before going to bed: "Now I lay me down to sleep, I pray the Lord my soul to keep. If I should die before I wake, I pray the Lord my soul to take." It seems likely that very few children who said this prayer were very concerned about dying during the night, but some adults remember being frightened by the idea of dying in their sleep. That prayer was later changed to: "Now I lay me down to sleep, I pray the Lord my soul to keep. Thy love be with me through the night and keep me till the morning light."

Changing attitudes about death education can be seen in the new endings of fairy tales and nursery rhymes. When a mother sings rock-a-by baby as she lulls her child to sleep, she probably never thinks about the last two lines of the rhyme, in which the bough breaks and the baby falls from the tree. When children were asked what happens to the baby in this verse, they said it was killed. Perhaps mothers who sing the lullaby just think of a baby falling from a low branch, or perhaps they just think about the warm and pleasant setting of the lullaby. In any case, Sandra L. Bertman, a well-known death educator, suggests that there is something lovely about beginning death education with a lullaby, for it is a warm and secure vantage point from which to peer out at harsh realities.

Many fairy tales and nursery rhymes deal with death. For example, the wolf eats Red Riding Hood, and Humpty Dumpty breaks when he falls from the wall. Death is removed from some of the modern versions of nursery rhymes, and, in many children's stories, everyone lives happily ever after, However, educators feel that children need not be protected from the idea of death. In fact, doing so only leads to the squeamishness and aversion that many adults feel about the subject.

When a pet dies, some parents try to distract their children by replacing the pet as quickly as possible. Now there is a new pet to love, and the sadness of death can be forgotten. But even though they may not express their sorrow about poor, dead Spot, children miss him and are curious about where he went. The new pet is not Spot. He is loved, but Spot is still loved, too.

Many teachers use the death of a child's pet or the death of a classroom pet as a springboard for discussions about feelings and questions about death and its effect on survivors. Even the young must experience sadness and disappointment in order to grow, and small doses of hardship in the early years help in dealing with death experiences in later years.

Protecting children from the horrors of death has long been the custom in the United States for many families. Young boys and girls have kept away from the traditional ceremonies and are still being told lies about what has happened to a loved one. Many parents feel that children will suffer less if they learn the truth gradually, but the opposite appears to be the case.

Timmy was a typical three-year-old who became very upset whenever he was separated from his mother or father. When his grandfather died, his parents decided to tell him that Grandpa had gone to the hospital, where he would stay until the doctors made him better. In time, they hoped that Timmy would forget about Grandpa and come to accept his absence as normal. However, Timmy heard people talking about how his grandfather had died. He knew that something was very wrong. Although Timmy was at an age when he could not understand that death is a permanent situation, telling Timmy fact rather than fiction is considered a better approach. Grandpa will never come back. Timmy may well believe that he can magically make Grandpa come back, but when he has been told the truth, trust in his parents will not be eroded, and he will be exposed to the concept of death as a part of life.

Karen was just six years old when her mother died, and she asked many questions about why her mother was no longer home. Her father told her that her mother had gone away on a trip, but Karen wondered why he cried so much about this. Aunt Sue told Karen that her mother was sick and would not be home for a long time. When Karen asked how long that would be, Aunt Sue rushed off to answer the phone.

Karen was taken to her cousin's house where she stayed for a few days. She had a good time there, for everyone seemed unusually nice to her. There were new toys, new dresses, and special treats. Even her cousin John, who often was very mean to her, was different. All of this would have been fun if people had not seemed so upset about her mother's "long trip" or "sickness."

After a week, Karen was taken back to her home, where she expected to see her mother. She was very upset when she found that her mother was not there. In answer to her questions, Karen's father admitted that her mother would never come back. He said that she had died and gone to heaven. Karen remembered that he had told her that her mother was just on a long trip. In Karen's mind, her visit to her cousin's was a long time, and she had fully expected her mother to be back when she returned home. How could she believe her father when he told lies? Where was heaven? If there were angels in heaven, would her mother become an angel? Certainly, her mother would come back before Christmas. Her father must be wrong. Her mother would not stay away at Christmastime. How could her mother have left without saying good-bye?

Karen had many questions and no one

seemed to be willing to answer them. It was a long time before Karen had some understanding of her mother's death. At night, when she cried for long periods of time, she wondered if she had caused her mother's death. Would her mother have died if she had picked up her toys without complaining? Did she cause her mother's death when she hit her with her ball? No one told Karen she had no part in what had happened to her mother. They treated her as if she were too young to understand. When a woman came to the house to live with them and take care of Karen, she was told that this was her new mother. Karen reacted by reverting to some of the baby habits she had outgrown. When she was punished for them, she felt that this was punishment because she had been responsible for her mother's death.

Many young children are "protected" from the death of a loved one by people who believe that they are doing the right thing. Adults, who feel uncomfortable about talking to anyone about death, may just avoid the subject when children ask questions. Experts feel that children's emotional growth is hindered by efforts to protect them from the realities

48

of death. They appear to be more capable of withstanding the stress that results from their limited understanding of death than of dealing with mystery and a sense of abandonment. In families where children are told the truth and are permitted to be part of the grieving, they appear to adjust to the situation more easily. They seem better prepared to deal with deaths of loved ones in the future than if the truth is hidden.

Telling a young child that a parent or sibling who has died has gone on a long journey is common. This is an attempt to ease the strain of the dead person's disappearance, but the child might interpret it to mean that the loved person has abandoned or deserted him or her without saying good-bye. When the person does not return, the child might feel that the person who died did not care enough about him or her to return.

Eight-year-old Danny was told that God took his father to heaven when he was just a young man because Daddy was so good. Danny was often told how good he was. He could not help wonder if God might take him, too. At night he wondered if a bogeyman was coming for him.

49

Before the age of ten, many children visualize death as an eerie ghost, a skeleton, or a bogeyman who comes to take the person who has died. As they grow older, they begin to understand more about the biological changes that take place when a person dies.

Why not just say that Grandma died because she was so sick? Jenny accepted this idea, but she was secretly frightened when she developed a serious case of the flu. Would she die?

Polly was told that her uncle had died and would be in a long sleep from which he would never awaken. Although many children are not bothered by this idea, some have been known to struggle very hard to stay awake at night for fear they will never awaken if they go to sleep. A fear of bedtime often develops in young children who connect sleep and death.

How can one tell a youngster about death without confusing or frightening the child? Suppose your mother or father dies and you want to comfort your younger sister. Children should be told the truth about the death immediately by the remaining parent or someone close, such as a brother or sister.

50

Sharing feelings of grief is the most meaningful kind of help that a relative can give. Young children need to know that adults have strong feelings, too. And they need to feel part of the family circle. Helping with simple activities, such as answering the phone, putting away coats for those who visit, and arranging flowers or storing gifts of food can help to relieve a child's anxiety at time of crisis.

All family members, friends, teachers, day care workers, and others who work with the child can help him or her to express their feelings. Just listening to the child can be important. Some children withdraw after a parent dies, some act out their angry feelings, and some react in a combination of these ways. You might make a child feel better by expressing your understanding of the fact that it takes a lot of emotional energy when a person is sad, but the sadness will not last forever. Being a good listener is one of the most helpful approaches. When comforting children and adults, what you say is not as important as showing, by listening, that you care.

CHAPTER

5

My glaſs is run

Dying the Good Death

From the very beginning of life, each living thing is marching toward death. Beginning as a single cell, each person grows and develops in his or her own special way from information coded in the genes and influences from the environment. Each person is unique, but just as certainly as one is born, one dies. Each death is unique, too. Some people experience peaceful deaths, while other deaths are violent. For some, death is welcome, while for others, it is the grim reaper.

Human beings are the only living things aware of the fact that they will die. In fact, some of us even imagine our own deaths or the deaths of friends or family. We imagine what it would be like for them if we died, or for us if it is their deaths we are imagining. Sometimes these fantasies are brought forth by the real death of someone we know. Other times they can be elicited out of anger or fear. In spite of these imaginings, our mortality and even the mortality of others is inconceivable. In the unconscious mind, one is immortal.

However, when patients reach terminal illness, they seem to know intuitively that they are going to die, and their mortality becomes very real. The greatest threat may then be fear of progressive isolation, the development of a sense of being alone. Death education, it is hoped, will help to make people more comfortable with those who are dying and teach them to overcome their apprehensions, doubts, and fears.

In earlier times, the dying old man or woman gathered the family at the bedside for the dramatic death bed scene in which he or she said good-bye to each one. Today, about 80 percent of the deaths in the United States take place in the hospital or nursing home. At the very end, death may not be serene. People gasp for air and choke to death. Those who suffer cardiac arrest in the hospital are surrounded by doctors and nurses who are struggling to revive the patient. Some die while in a coma, and no one knows what is going on in their minds, if anything. According to physicians, bleeding to death is not too unpleasant for the patient. Dying in one's sleep seems peaceful enough, although in most such cases, no one observes the final minutes.

"The good death" is often a description of the person before the final moments. Many patients who are well along the road toward death, accept it with equanimity. We say they die a good death, but there is no single way to do this.

Dying a good death may depend on how one prepares for it. Many individuals suffer a great deal of mental anguish because they and their relatives do not know how to react with one another at such a time. For those who know, or suspect, that they are dying, there may be much emotional pain in addition to physical pain. Families and friends can do a great deal to ease their burdens if they are willing to learn about death and try to understand the feelings of the dying.

57

Much the same is true for the individuals who are approaching death.

Consider the case of Sara. She is in the hospital after an operation for cancer of the pancreas. Although she knows that she is very sick and suspects she may never get better, she takes pleasure in selecting the color for the carpeting of the house that she and her husband are building. She has read about the short time that people live after cancer is discovered in the pancreas, but death happens to other people. She is only thirty years old, and not many people die at that age. Even though the doctor has told her that her chances of surviving a year are slim, Sara cannot believe him. Unconsciously, she believes she is immortal. At this point, she is unable to accept her own death. She is in the first stage of dying, one known as denial.

According to Dr. Elisabeth Kübler-Ross, a well-known psychiatrist who is considered an authority on matters of death and dying, denial functions as a buffer when one hears something shocking. Denial gives people time to collect themselves. With time, they can mobilize other, less radical defenses. Denial may be present from time to time as

58

patients who have reached an acceptance of their own death find the need to return to the pursuit of life.

In a few weeks after her operation, Sara moved from denial to the next stage of dying—she began to accept the reality of her illness. After the typical reaction of telling herself, "No, it cannot be me," Sara replaced the denial with feelings of anger and resentment. Normally, she was a mild, pleasant person, but now she raged against the nurses, her doctor, and her family. This anger and resentment were part of a normal reaction, one that typically follows the denial phase. "Why me?" she asked herself again and again. She thought of her old aunt who was alone day after day, uninterested in anything around her. She seemed to be waiting to die. Sara had things to do, including living in her new house where she planned to enjoy being active in the new community.

Sara's family found it difficult to understand the change in her personality. She was never an angry, complaining person, and they were doing everything possible to make her comfortable. No one looked at the situation from her point of view. They were no

59

different from most people who find this second stage of dying an especially difficult time.

In the next phase of dying, the terminally ill patient uses bargaining. Unconsciously, Sara felt that she might make better progress with God if she appealed nicely for a reprieve. If she could only live long enough to spend one year in her house, she would work harder than ever on the committee for abused children. Like most other terminally ill patients, Sara made her bargain with God secretly. Hospital chaplains and religious leaders who visit the dying are told of such bargains. According to Dr. Kübler-Ross, these promises are often connected with some kind of guilt. She suggests that hospital chaplains and doctors who become aware of bargains pursue the reasons for them and relieve patients of irrational fears and wishes for punishment.

Early stages of dying are eventually replaced by feelings of depression. Many unpleasant factors enter into the life of a person as terminal illness proceeds. There may be disfiguration of the body, financial problems due to medical bills, job losses, difficult family situations, especially where mothers can no longer care for their young children, and numerous other problems that add to the general sadness.

Sara, who was always proud of her beautiful hair, tried to laugh when she looked in the mirror to adjust her new wig, but she found it difficult to accept the loss of her hair, which had fallen out by the handfuls after her radiation treatments began. She also suffered a great deal from vomiting and from pain, but when she complained, it was mainly about not being available to make decisions concerning the new house. Her husband had always depended on her judgment about colors of paint, placement of furniture, landscaping, and other procedures that were now taking place without Sara's input. In addition to being depressed because she could not function in her role as wife, Sara was suffering from the depression that comes with preparing herself for the final separation from this world.

Depression was followed by the stage known as acceptance. By now, Sara had worked through her anguish and anxieties, and she was ready to die. She had grown very

61

weak, slept a great deal, and wished that her family and her doctors would stop promising that she would improve. They told her that new treatments might reduce the size of the tumor at a time when her body was so filled with cancer that she knew this would not matter. She was ready to let go, and, after a discussion, she and her husband agreed to tell the doctor that it was time to stop all attempts to prolong her life. She slept much of the time, and she expressed her desire to have the hospital refuse visitors other than her husband. She was not happy, nor was she sad. She showed little interest in anything, but seemed comforted by the presence of her husband. Sara was reaching the end with peace and dignity.

Not everyone goes through the stages of dying described by Dr. Kübler-Ross. Sudden death from accidents, suicide, and murder prevent this, and for many terminally ill who spend a long time dying, the good death comes after a fight to the very end. There are many cases in which patients have been given only a short time to live, but they have proved their doctors wrong. Books such as *Anatomy of an Illness* by Norman Cousins and *Love,*

Medicine and Miracles by Bernie S. Siegel give examples of the relationship between attitude and disease. In general, patients who are confident they can beat a disease appear to have a better chance of recovery than those who resign themselves to a prolonged illness and death. Many doctors accept as fact the idea that a person's attitude plays a part in healing. The mind has an effect on bodily functions, but even though many people live far longer than statistics would have predicted, they all must meet death. The style of dying is an individual thing. Good deaths need not involve the five steps mentioned in the story of Sara.

Although relatively few children die, many who do seem to have an intuitive sense about their nearness to death and tend to have fewer fears than adults. Children who had cancer have coauthored a book with their caregivers, *There Is a Rainbow Behind Every Dark Cloud,* in which they note that it seemed easier to talk about dying with other children than with adults. They felt that adults often seemed nervous, changed the subject, and told them they should not think of things like death. Fifteen-year-old Mary, for example, thinks about death every day, for she knows her own death will come soon. She is suffering from leukemia, and she feels frightened. Mary's mother pretends that she will get well, but Mary wishes she would talk about what is really happening. Mary wrote her the following note in an effort to break the ice:

Mother, you know I am dying, but you leave the room when I try to talk about it. I know you care about me, but I am afraid you are avoiding me because you might cry during your visit. I can tell you have been crying a great deal at home because your eyes are red when you come to the hospital. Maybe it would be better if we could cry together.

Please do not go away so you can cry alone. I would rather have you here holding my hand. I need to have you here when I die. I have never died before. I love you very much.

Mary

In their book, the children reported that talking with their peers was found to be helpful.

64

Drawing pictures about death and talking about it made it less scary. One child drew a picture of a large sun and said that death was like being in the light everywhere. In the summary of their book, the children said they learned that letting go of the past and forgiving everyone and everything helped them to be less afraid of death.

One new way that seems to help young people meet death is the use of video tapes to record experiences and thoughts. A study of the value of this procedure showed that making video tapes helped dying young people to feel more in control of their lives. Many children expressed hope for continued life, even though they had been told that there was little chance that they would live for more than a few months, or even a year. Others expressed relief at being given "permission to die" by parents who had formerly been afraid to admit that their death was near. One child said she felt she had an obligation to stay alive, but she was afraid she could no longer fill that obligation. When her parents talked to her about her inevitable death, she felt she could die in peace.

No one knows if it is better to fight death

till the very end or to prepare for it and accept it. One does not really get to choose the time and kind of death, except in cases of suicide. According to Eastern wisdom, the answer to the question, "How long is it good for a man to live?" is "As long as he prefers life over death." In the case of suicide, the desire for death is usually temporary. Counselors who provide hope may save lives, but for those in extreme physical pain with no hope of recovery, death is a good friend.

The aversion of the well for those who are dying has been mentioned earlier. Both doctors and families tend to abandon the terminally ill at a time when they desperately need kind words, affectionate touching, and verbal expressions of love. In the past two decades, the hospice movement has grown rapidly as an effort to replace the cold, clinical hospital death with "an old-fashioned death." A hospice is a team approach in which there is an effort to provide medical, social, psychological, and spiritual support for both the dying patient and the family. Patients frequently express wishes to die at a home, or in a homelike setting, and welcome the attempts of hospice workers to help them work

66

through the stages of dying. However, doctors warn that patients must consider the possibility that hospital treatment may afford years of extended survival. They suggest that one should consider a second opinion before selecting a terminal care situation where there is no aggressive medical treatment.

Hospices offer a place to die, either in one's own home, or in a special home for dying people, with a goal of making them as comfortable as possible. In contrast to hospitals and nursing homes, where the goal is curing the patient, a hospice is concerned with the quality of life of the dying.

"Hospice" is a medieval term for a way station where travelers could rest. Later the term was applied to places where nuns cared for the dying. Some of today's hospices are special places within a hospital, but many of them are located in separate buildings. People who live in a hospice connected with a nursery school program feel especially fortunate. Children visit the dying, accept their conditions, and receive love and attention from the residents, who, in turn enjoy visits from the young. In many communities, the hospice movement consists only of staff

67

members and/or trained volunteers devoted to the home care of patients.

Hospice care is not about death and dying, according to leaders of the movement. It is about life and living. Several thousand hospice programs are now functioning in the United States and about two hundred of them are supplying care for children.

In the drama of death, new approaches consider the roles of family, medical staff, and the dying patient, increasing chances that the ending will be a good death. The good death is the crowning glory to a good life.

CHAPTER
6

There is rest in Heaven.

Death by Suicide

Homicide and suicide vie as the second most common cause of death among the young, the first being accidents. While it is difficult to determine the number of suicides, it has been estimated that an adolescent in America attempts suicide every seventy-eight seconds, and one succeeds every ninety minutes. Until recently suicide was a topic that few people would discuss. It evoked feelings of guilt in those whose lives were touched. They felt that a suicide in the family was shameful. But the increasing suicide rate and heavy media coverage have been responsible for more open discussion of the subject.

Suicide rates have increased dramatically

71

among young adults, and there are predictions that there will be a 95 percent increase in the fifteen to twenty-four age group by the year 2000. Reports of suicide among young children are rare, but these, too, appear to be increasing. Perhaps this is because they are being recognized more often than in previous years. Child psychiatrists say they are observing more suicidal behavior in children as young as five and six, and there is much more recognition of suicidal thinking in this age group.

In one study, researchers concluded that 87 percent of the poison cases in children over six were deliberate and not accidental. Young children have been known to bring about their own deaths by strangling themselves with a variety of cords and ropes. Others take their lives by playing tag among cars on busy streets, stabbing, burning, cutting, and scalding themselves, as well as by jumping from high places.

Jenny tried many kinds of self-destructive behavior. She ran in front of cars, cut herself with scissors, crawled into a clothes dryer, and jumped from high places. Her psychiatrist believed that she acted this way because her parents were abusing her. She abused herself because she was angry, but could not abuse her parents. Her suicide threats and attempts were studied in a clinic that specializes in learning about self-destructive behavior. Unfortunately, many children's cries for help end in death because they are not heard.

An estimated six thousand or more teenagers kill themselves, and as many as a million young people make suicide attempts each year. Experts believe some factors that cause young people to flirt with death are family problems, drug abuse, lack of job opportunities, and the availability of guns. Many experts see suicide as the end of a breakdown that begins with the use of alcohol and other drugs to drown out emotional pain.

Feelings of hopelessness and helplessness are widely acknowledged as warning signs of suicide. These were present for many years before Peter took his life.

Peter was a young man of twenty who lived with his parents. He had completed high school, but he dropped out of college. Each time he started a new job, he quit after a few months. Peter was certain that he could not

73

please his boss. In fact, he felt he could not do much of anything. He even had trouble making friends.

Peter was seeing a therapist who was helping him to sort out his problems, but Peter felt that he was not making any progress. He tried to take his life several times by taking an overdose of his medication, but, each time, his mother found out what had happened and called for help. He was rushed to the hospital, where his stomach was pumped out. Peter felt that he could not even take his own life without messing up.

The therapist, who was trying to help Peter become independent, suggested that he move into his own apartment. He told Peter how to apply for financial aid and helped him find a place that would be his own. Peter had mixed feelings about leaving home. On the night before he was going to move, Peter had an idea. He could pretend that he was excited about his new apartment, but as soon as he moved, he would take an overdose of pills, and, since his mother would not be there to find out, he would succeed in this suicide attempt.

Peter had already arranged for his funeral

and paid for three cemetery lots. One lot would be his last resting place, and the other two would be places for his parents. When his parents discovered what he had done, they would know that he really loved them. Usually, Peter was sorry for the pain he had caused them, but sometimes he wanted to punish them for not understanding how awful he really felt. He just could not live with his sorrow anymore. Suicide in the apartment was a sure way to end the pain.

Peter visited his therapist the evening before he moved, but he was careful not to mention his plans. The therapist was pleased to find Peter in such a relaxed mood and felt that the move toward independence was responsible. Actually, Peter felt calm the evening before he moved because he knew he had a solution to his problems.

After Peter's parents helped him move his clothing and his furniture to the new apartment, they left him in a good mood and promised to call him in the morning. Although they did not know it, he really felt rather sad because he knew he would never see them again. However, he was ready to put his plan into action. He wrote a note to his mother, telling her to be glad for him. He really wanted to stop the pain of his depression, and death was the only way he could be sure of accomplishing that. She must try to understand. He wrote a note to his father, too, asking him to take care of his mother and to help her find a support group to help her understand what he had done. Then Peter took all the pills in the bottles that held his prescriptions.

No one answered the phone when Peter's mother tried to call him the next morning. She tried several times, and then she asked the superintendent of the building to check the apartment to see if her son was sick. He found Peter lying in his bed, but it was too late to send him to the hospital for emergency treatment.

Peter's death seemed sudden, even though he had tried suicide several times before he succeeded. His mother blamed herself for letting him move. She just could not make herself believe that Peter would have succeeded in taking his life if he had continued to live at home.

The guilt feelings that Peter's mother felt were typical of those suffered by families and friends of anyone who commits suicide. Although they try to find some comfort in the thought that this is what the person wanted, they cannot help thinking that there must have been a way to stop it.

Many suicides are averted by calls for help to suicide prevention centers by friends and relatives who know the warning signs of suicide. Prevention programs often use young people as their eyes and ears, telling them what to look for and what to do if they think someone close might be at risk. No one wants to believe that a friend or relative is considering death, but knowing the signs of suicidal thinking and contacting a hotline has saved many lives.

Here are some of the warning signs:

Remarks that indicate a person feels depressed and is suffering from low self-esteem, such as "You would be better off without me," or "You don't care if I'm alive or dead." There is no truth in the idea that threats of suicide mean a person will not act. Just the opposite is true. Suicide threats are one of the warning signs. Here are others:

- Setting one's affairs in order.

77

- Giving away possessions.

- A definite suicide plan. "You can't stop me," is a way of saying, "Please stop me."

- Remarks about hopelessness and helplessness, such as: "I'll never get better"; "I can't do anything right"; "Leave me alone, I want to die"; "You would be better off if I were dead."

- Estrangement from family.

If you recognize any of the above cries for help, contact a crisis intervention center, a suicide prevention center, or your local hospital. Assuring a suicidal person that everything will be all right seems like an empty promise to those who feel that their situation is hopeless. Daring a person to carry out a suicide threat increases the risk. By listening to their problems and offering understanding to those who believe death is the only solution for their pain, you can help to keep people alive until they learn that bad times come, but they also go.

Youth suicide is a national problem that

strikes every level of society. It can be solved only by combined efforts of individuals, organizations, and government.

In recent years, clusters of suicides among young people have occurred in various parts of the United States. No one knows just why this is happening, but most experts feel that talking with teens about suicide and providing information is one of the best ways of prevention. New studies confirm the idea that education about suicide does not increase the rate of suicide, but appears to decrease it. On the other hand, reading or hearing about the actual suicide of a famous person, or being in the same school or community where suicides occur, appears to "give permission" to young people who are already feeling troubled and confused. Hearing about these suicides appears to push those already at risk closer to taking action.

In many high schools where "copycat" suicides have occurred, immediate programs of prevention have been put into effect. School psychologists and community counselors start group counseling while the school schedule continues. The routine of classes makes young people more secure. Students who are having problems are permitted to leave class to see counselors, and students who are believed to be at high risk are called in promptly to talk with the crisis workers after the tragedy has occurred.

In addition to intervention programs, suicide prevention groups are spreading throughout the entire country. Steps can be taken to help those who believe that death is the only answer to their problems. As more people become aware of these steps, it is hoped that the number of suicides will decrease.

Every suicide has a distinct effect on the family, friends, and community, and some aspects of their grief are unique. It is especially difficult for them to express their thoughts, and often they do not want to talk about the suicide. Perhaps this is because many people feel some extra blame, or guilt, about the death, even though none may be involved. Their silence is considered an attempt to keep a cap on these feelings. This can prevent a working through of mourning.

Refusal to talk about a suicide in the family and attempts to hide it from others is often called a Grand Bargain. In *Silent Grief: Liv-*

ing in the Wake of Suicide, Christopher Lukas and Henry M. Seiden describe the case of
a girl, Bernice, whose family told her and two
siblings that their eighteen-year-old brother
had died from lung cancer. They were hiding
the fact that the true cause of his death was
suicide. As long as eleven years later, Bernice
was troubled by feelings that her parents had
betrayed her. She suffered from severe depression and had also attempted suicide. Her
sister and young brother had serious medical
problems that may well have been connected
with the silence about their brother's suicide.

Bernice told her therapist that her family
had a party on the eleventh anniversary of
her brother's suicide, but his name was never
mentioned. This family made a bargain, believing that if one does not talk about the
suicide, there is no need to deal with it. Their
idea that silent healing will prevent anger
and guilt from surfacing was actually a
costly one.

When a loved one has committed suicide,
many survivors respond by taking action after a period of mourning. They join self-help
groups in which they share their grief and
overcome feelings of stigma and shame, and

81

this sharing of experiences provides comfort. Group members help one another and heal themselves as they help.

In many areas, self-help groups can be located by contacting a mental health association, a clinic, or a hospital. In some areas, a group known as The Compassionate Friends has branches that specialize in helping survivors deal with the painful aftermath of suicide.

CHAPTER 7

HERE LYES THE BODY

Playing God

argory was driving home from a tennis match when a drunken driver came speeding toward her and smashed into her car. In court, the driver explained that he was trying to commit suicide. Margory had been a vibrant teenager with potential for a fine future. She was robbed of that future by the driver of the car that caused her brain to die. Although her breathing continued, Margory, as a person, was dead, kept "alive" by sophisticated machines.

Death can be thought of as a series of deaths. This is well illustrated by the case of a pregnant woman who suffered from seizures that were followed by brain death. She met the definition of death suggested by the American Bar Association that states: "For all legal purposes, a human body with irreversible cessation of total brain function, according to usual and customary standards of medical practice shall be considered dead." The Uniform Determination of Death Act states: "An individual who has sustained either (1) irreversible cessation of circulatory and respiratory functions, or (2) irreversible cessation of all functions of the entire brain, including the brain stem, is dead." This definition of death was proposed by the President's Commission for the Study of Ethical Problems in Medicine and Biomedical and Behavioral Research and endorsed by the American Medical Association and the American Bar Association.

The pregnant woman qualified by both of the above definitions, but what about the fetus? It weighed only one pound, so it was doubtful that the child would survive an emergency caesarean section. Even if the baby lived, there was the probability of mental retardation and many physical difficulties. With the encouragement of the family, the decision was made to keep the mother on a respirator to supply the oxygen that her heart needed to retain her vital organs and the placenta that was nourishing the baby. Nine weeks later, when careful monitoring revealed that the fetus had stopped growing, doctors delivered a three pound, three ounce boy by caesarean section. His chances of survival were considered excellent. After the baby was delivered, the woman's husband spent an hour alone with her in a small private room. Then the tubes were removed, and she died a second death. In describing this case, the Hastings Center titled their article, "On Dying More Than One Death."

As medical science develops more ways of keeping people alive, an increasing number of patients become part of a controversy about the right to die. The medical professions are dedicated to restoring health and preventing death, so it is not surprising to find that many caregivers feel a sense of frustration and failure when death approaches. Discontinuing life support seems an admission of failure. However, in many cases, continued life support is no longer a benefit to the patient.

One of the most famous cases involving the

question of continued life support was that of Karen Ann Quinlan. This young lady was admitted to a hospital on April 14, 1975. Her breathing had stopped, and she was placed on a respirator when mouth-to-mouth resuscitation failed. Doctors decided she had taken a tranquilizer and drunk a quantity of alcohol, which caused her to sink into the unconscious state. Irreversible brain damage made it impossible for her to breathe without the help of a machine to force air into her lungs. The dying process was prolonged until June 11, 1985, even though her parents won a landmark court battle to have the respirator disconnected in 1976. By that time, her body had recovered enough to regulate her breathing without the respirator. However, many would say that Karen Ann Quinlan died as a person at the beginning of the coma, not ten years later, when she lay in the fetal position and weighed just sixty pounds. She had not made meaningful contact with the world in that decade.

Karen Ann Quinlan's death focused attention on social attitudes toward death. The quality of human life versus the length of human life became a topic that is now discussed quite openly and quite often.

While debates about heroic measures to prolong life continue, many individuals are not permitted to make decisions for themselves. Consider the case of Mrs. Smith, who was eighty years old when she begged the medical team caring for her in the hospital to let her die. Nevertheless, life-sustaining tubes were inserted into her nose, her throat, and her arms. She tried to unfasten them, but each time she succeeded in disconnecting a tube, it was replaced. Soon, she withdrew into a private world and never spoke again, perhaps because her life was so intolerable. Three years later, she died.

Cases such as Mrs. Smith's are the subject of many conferences including discussions about patients who want to die. Hard-won progress makes it possible in some states for terminally ill people to refuse respirators and other life-prolonging measures.

Suppose a person can no longer communicate with the medical staff? In some states, the next of kin, or a person with a Durable Power of Attorney is permitted to make such a decision. But plans must be made in advance.

At the Jones house, the family gathered in the den to discuss the subject of Living Wills. These are documents that people sign while they are still healthy, making known their wishes in case a decision must be made about prolonging treatment when they are dying. Grammy and Grandpa explained that they had signed Living Wills that gave instructions about the kind of medical care they would want and not want, in case they could no longer express their own wishes. They gave copies to their lawyer, their doctor, and several members of the family. In their effort to make certain that their wishes were carried out, they gave their son, Jonathan, a Durable Power of Attorney, legally allowing him the authority to speak for each of them if one or both could not do so.

Jonathan said they were asking him to play God. At first, he was not sure that he wanted the responsibility they had given him. He did not want to feel that he was responsible for the death of one of his parents. At this point, their son Toby suggested that God was not keeping people alive with life support machines, the doctors were.

After Jonathan realized that he would have the help of the hospital's ethics committee in making a decision, he felt comfortable about the part he might someday have to play in the care of his parents. He even felt good knowing that he could help give his parents the privilege of dying with grace and dignity rather than suffering through years of pain from diseases that gradually destroy mind and body.

The members of the medical profession are dedicated to restoring health and forestalling death, but what about "letting die?" The American Medical Association issued the following opinion in 1986:

For humane reasons, with informed consent, a physician may do what is medically necessary to alleviate severe pain, or cease or omit treatment to permit a terminally ill patient whose death is imminent to die. However, he should not intentionally cause death. In deciding whether the administration of potentially life-prolonging medical treatment

91

is in the best interest of the patient who is incompetent to act in his own behalf, the physician should determine what the possibility is for extending life under humane and comfortable conditions and what are the prior expressed wishes of the patient and attitudes of the family or those who have responsibility for the custody of the patient.[1]

However, in many types of cases the above statement does not help physicians and the families of patients who must make decisions. One can make a rational case of withholding food and water from a patient, but this is still a very emotional issue. And if a patient expresses the wish to die, is it right to withhold nourishment? The case of Elizabeth Bouvia, a twenty-eight-year-old quadriplegic, is a case in point. She asked the staff of the convalescent hospital in which she had been a patient for years to stop feeding her. The case went to court, but her wishes were not granted. Although Elizabeth Bouvia contended that she was not trying to commit

[1]*Current Opinions,* section 2.18, p. 13.

suicide, the court insisted that she be force fed. Since her medical condition made life extremely difficult and painful for her, many people felt that her request was reasonable.

Controversy about the right to die for patients in various situations continues, with court rulings that vary widely. Organizations such as the Society for the Right to Die and Concern for the Dying provide literature about this problem. Certainly, there are no easy answers for the patients and for the families of people who are faced with decisions of life and death as the new world of medical technology confronts them with choices in which they feel they are playing God.

CHAPTER
8

Caring for the Dead

After a person dies, family or friends must decide what to do with the body. If there is no one to plan and pay for a "decent burial," the body is disposed of in a public burial ground, often called potter's field, from a biblical story. In New York City, bodies are placed in pine coffins, then loaded onto a truck that drives to the ferry dock, boards the ferry, and delivers the coffins to Hart Island. There, a detail of prison inmates buries the dead in potter's field.

On any one day at potter's field in New York, there are likely to be two dozen or more pine boxes that contain adults, newborns, and fetuses. Some of the coffins are marked with names of the dead, while others just give the sex and information about whether or not the corpse was an adult, child, or baby. The loads are bigger in cold weather when some of the homeless freeze to death on the street. After burial, the tombs are marked with foot-tall concrete blocks.

Even though the dead in the graves at potter's field are unknown and often unidentified, many people who work there show respect for them. Inmates and supervisors alike wonder why no one cared about these people, and they feel that they are contributing something by burying their bodies.

In great contrast to the burials at potter's field are the elaborate funeral arrangements directed by undertakers. Today, there is considerable objection to some of the euphemisms of the funeral trade, such as "slumber parlor" (viewing room), "reposing room" (where the body is prepared), "floral tributes" (flowers), "coaches" or "professional cars" (hearses). These words tend to hide the reality of death, when many people feel that one purpose of a funeral is to play a part in bringing this reality home.

Some undertakers are unwilling or reluctant to provide simple services at low cost.

Jessica Mitford alerted the public to the commercial aspects of burials through her book *The American Way of Death,* in 1963. She expressed the view that the funeral trade was extracting too much money from the bereaved at a time when they could not make wise decisions because of emotional stress. Even though Jessica Mitford's book had a strong influence on malpractices, many people who have little money for the necessities of life still buy expensive caskets, burial plots, memorial stones, clothing and cosmetics for the viewing, and large quantities of flowers to express their love for the person who has died. Some poor people put a few dollars each week into an insurance policy so they can be certain of an elegant burial.

Most bereaved relatives are in such a state of shock and grief after a death that they accept whatever a funeral director suggests is proper and acceptable. One must remember that funeral directors are in business to make a profit, as well as to make a difficult time easier for the family of the person who died, and to provide a pleasant, or even beautiful, setting in which to experience loss and grief.

Various funeral directors approach the sit-

99

uation differently. Not all funeral directors (morticians) arrange a funeral according to what the people can afford, but for some it is common practice. Federal and state governments have taken steps to curb abuses and now require itemized price disclosures before arrangements are made. Laws forbid the claim that embalming, caskets, and burial vaults can preserve the body for a long time. Such regulations were the result of increased public resistance to the commercialization of death.

Death ceremonies, when wisely planned, are important in meeting the needs of family and friends, for they are part of the process of healing grief. In recent years, there has been a trend toward less elaborate funerals and more emphasis on meaningful ways of saying good-bye. The amount of money spent on funeral arrangements may have little to do with how well the funeral meets the needs of the survivors.

The simplest approach to caring for the body after death may be very meaningful, according to Lisa Carlson, author of the book *Caring for Your Own Dead,* which describes do-it-yourself burials and cremations. The author, who buried her husband without an undertaker, feels that the favorable economics of this method are secondary to the emotional benefits that were derived. However, this route is not practical or appealing to most people. They prefer to let an undertaker deal with the body.

In several hundred cities in the United States memorial societies have been formed to help people plan in advance for simple funerals at low cost. These are nonprofit groups that encourage people to write down their wishes for their own body disposition and death ceremonies.

Along with the trend away from elaborate funerals is the trend toward disposal of the dead by cremation, a process in which bodies are reduced to ashes and bone fragments through intense heat. As cemeteries moved away from the immediate community to less valuable land, the practice of visiting the graves of loved ones grew less frequent. In some cases, caskets were moved from old cemeteries in city areas long after burial took place, to make room for urban centers. This lack of a guarantee of a permanent burial site and the practical aspect of cremation in-

101

creased the trend toward what many people consider to be a clean, orderly process for returning a human body to the elements.

Cremation was practiced as long ago as 1000 B.C. and continued through the years in various places and times. For example, at one time the Greeks cremated bodies because they believed that the flames set the soul free. The ancient Romans practiced both earth burial and cremation. Today, most religions permit cremation, but, in some cases, special permission is needed for this type of burial. The ashes are clean and white and may be stored indefinitely in a container. Many families prefer to scatter the dead person's ashes in a favorite spot, such as a garden, the sea, or a ski slope. A few states have laws that prohibit the scattering of ashes, but these laws serve no aesthetic or hygienic purpose.

Each society has developed ways of caring for the dead, with ceremonies and rituals that help to integrate death into the lives of those who remain. Death ceremonies in the United States usually consist of a funeral service, one that is held in the presence of the body, with the casket open or closed, or a memorial service that is held after the body has been

102

removed. Sometimes a graveside ceremony takes place in addition to or instead of a previous service.

Caring for the dead dates back at least as far as Neanderthal man, and the variety of funeral practices has been wide. Among the most studied are the customs of the Egyptians, for their elaborate death rites included great efforts to preserve the body. At one period, Egyptians believed that the soul would live in Paradise only so long as the body survived on the earth. Beliefs about the afterlife changed many times during the course of Egyptian history, but, at one period, the inclusion of things needed for the afterlife was carried to extreme. In some cases, a whole suite of tomb chambers was needed to house the articles.

In Egypt and in many other countries, preservation practices varied with the status and wealth of the dead person, and some procedures were elaborate. For example, many bodies were purged and then eviscerated while they soaked for seventy days in a solution of chemicals, such as bicarbonate of soda. This dissolved the tissues, and nothing was left but skin and bone. Another procedure was the surgical removal of internal organs. The viscera and the brain were preserved separately in jars and buried along with the body. The empty cavities were washed and, after spices had been put into them, sewn together. When they had soaked for seventy days in soda, the bodies were carefully wrapped in yards of cotton or linen, in the fashion of mummies in museums today.

A great variety of other embalming procedures were used during the ages, but the practice of arterial embalming was not used on a large scale until the end of the nineteenth century. In this procedure, blood is drained from the body and replaced with a solution containing formalin. Embalming sometimes includes sanitizing the body through disinfection, dressing it, and restoring it to make it socially presentable for public appearance, but this is not always the case. In the Jewish religion, it is customary to bury the dead as soon as possible, since no embalming is permitted.

Medical embalmers preserved the bodies of some soldiers on the battlefields of the Civil War so that they could be sent home to the family burial grounds. It was the embalming of the body of Abraham Lincoln that brought the practice to the attention of large numbers of Americans. His body was so well embalmed in 1865 that it could still be viewed in 1899 and was said to be in a perfect state of preservation.

There are numerous embalming fluids and cosmetics that can help to make the body appear lifelike for those who wish to say a last good-bye. Such viewings, with the "laying out" of the dead in an open casket, are becoming less popular in the United States, although there is still a great deal of emphasis on bringing the body home. In the United States there is little active participation by the family or friends other than attendance at services.

Cremation of the body is not as common as earth burial in the United States. However, elsewhere in the world cremation is an important part of the death services. In much of India and South Asia, cremation takes place after the body has been carried by mourners to a level area on a river bank close to a temple. The body is burned on a pile of logs, and the ashes are thrown into the river. The biggest event in the life of a person of Hindu

105

faith is death. If possible, a dying person travels to the holy city of Benares to bathe in the sacred river, the Ganges, so he can become free of sins. Although the city seems to be bustling with death, there is a holiday atmosphere among Hindus, who regard death as the end of a tiresome journey.

In the past, Hindu widows practiced a ritual known as suttee, or sati, which required a woman to throw herself on the funeral pyre of her husband. From earliest childhood, girls were taught to think of their husbands as godlike figures, and that suttee was the ultimate achievement for a girl. This practice was outlawed in 1829, although it still occurs occasionally. Many widows of Hindu faith shave off their hair and wait for death to come to them.

A Moslem funeral prepares the dead person for the angels, who are believed to interrogate the corpse. After the body is washed, the hands are arranged for prayer, and the entire corpse is enshrouded. The body is often buried without a coffin, so that it may sit up for the angels.

Christians, Jews, and many others believe that the soul leaves the body of the dead per-

106

son for a life hereafter. Religious services and/or memorial services are followed by a commitment, or committal service, at the graveside or place of burial of the ashes. Family members usually participate by reading poems, prayers, and/or dropping flowers or earth into the grave.

Although the ways of caring for the bodies of the dead differ widely, death ceremonies provide a source of stength and encouragement for those who must look to the future without the presence of a beloved person.

CHAPTER
9

Sacred

Grief and Mourning

"You cannot prevent the birds of sorrow from flying over your head, but you can prevent them from nesting in your hair," is an old Chinese proverb that is still true. Even though some farewells are said at the death bed or the funeral, the process of saying good-bye, or mourning, may last months or even years. Grief cannot be hurried, but it decreases with time. The period known as mourning brings the strong emotions under control so that a person may feel whole again in spite of the death of someone close. Through mourning, one can work back to productive living, even though some sorrows lasts forever.

People respond to death in a wide variety of

ways, and there is no right or wrong way to feel. The nature and extent of sorrow depends on many things, such as how one is related to the person who died, the role of that person in the life of the mourner, the way one handles any kind of crisis, and the circumstances of the death.

Vicky was relieved when her mother died. She had said good-bye to her two whole years before, when she had the stroke that took away her ability to relate to anybody or anything. Once a week, Vicky's father took her to the hospital to sit at the bedside of the woman who lay there quietly. Vicky kept telling herself that this used to be her mother, but the days they had enjoyed together seemed so far away. Day after day, she tried talking to her mother in the hope that she would show some sign of recognition, but the vacant stare never changed.

Although Vicky had many good memories of the days when her mother was well, the last two years had been very difficult for everyone in the family. Sometimes Vicky felt a little guilty about being glad when her mother died. But the counselor at school told Vicky that it was not wrong to feel the way she did. There was nothing terrible about it. She reminded Vicky of the many good feelings about the talks she and her mother had before she lapsed into a coma. Vicky had grieved when her mother first became unconscious. Her mourning was over by the time her mother died.

College student Tommy Singer never had a chance to say good-bye to his sister, Susan, before she died. Tommy had been waiting for Susan at the finish line of a bike race, wondering why she did not come in with the first group of bikers, when he began to wonder if something was wrong. Susan was fast and usually she won. When the last racers straggled in without her, Tommy was certain that something terrible had happened. He asked a friend if she had seen Susan, and a stranger who overheard the question told him about the girl who had been struck by a car near the beginning of the race.

Tommy could not believe that a car had crossed the race area at full speed. He could not believe that Susan would not come riding toward him on her bike within the next few minutes. How could he believe that she would never ride her bike again?

113

Tommy soon learned that the medical crew had reached Susan almost at once after the accident and that she had died in the ambulance on the way to the hospital. Now, he must go there to make arrangements for the release of her body and its journey by plane to the town where he and Susan had been born.

Tommy felt numb. He acted without thinking about what he was doing. Later, he remembered breaking the news to his mother by phone, and her stunned silence. He remembered reaching neighbors, who promised to care for his mother until he reached home. Almost automatically, he had packed some clothing and caught the next plane.

The next few days seemed like a nightmare. Mrs. Singer was in such a state of shock that she could not talk to anyone, so Tommy made all the arrangements for the services and the burial. He was the one who received friends and relatives at the funeral home, and he found support in this.

Looking back over those first days, Tommy wondered how he had completed the tasks that needed to be done. He knew that his mind kept denying Susan's death, but he re-

114

membered learning in a class on death education that denial is nature's way of warding off the full impact of a trauma until the body can absorb it.

After the rituals of the wake and the funeral were over, Tommy suffered even greater pain. He had always felt invulnerable. Bad things only happened to other people, but that was no longer true. Would something happen to his mother? To him? He felt frightened, sad, confused, and angry. Although Tommy did not realize it, this was all part of what is known as grief work. So were the physical symptoms: lack of appetite, exhaustion, sleeplessness, diminished sex drive.

Tommy was surprised by the intensity of his anger at the drunken driver who had killed his sister. He tried to think rationally, but he found it hard to control his feelings. Tommy grew angry at the people who ran the race, the medical workers who had tried to save his sister, and even at his mother for permitting his sister to participate in bicycle races. One part of him knew that he was not making sense. But it helped to scream out loud, write letters to the driver of the car

115

(which Tommy never mailed), and jog even farther than usual.

Lurking beneath Tommy's anger was a terrible sadness, which he now began to face. He kept wondering if there was something he had done to cause Susan's death. He knew that this is typical of people who are experiencing grief after the death of a loved one, but that did not make it much easier. Tommy thought of the many times he had wished that his sister were dead. He had even told her so the last time they had an argument. He knew that most of his guilt feelings were not realistic, and he finally forgave himself for those that were.

Susan kept appearing in Tommy's dreams. Every now and then, he would expect her to come into the room, just as she had so many times when they had lived at home together. There were sudden flashes of some of the happy times they had together, memories of laughing, teasing, and caring. The days gradually became easier, and he began to think more about his own life and his plans for the future.

Tommy could now actively confront the feelings and thoughts that his sister's death provoked. He would never forget his sister, but he knew that his own life had been strengthened by his ability to deal with death and build a more positive philosophy of life.

Tommy's mother had a more difficult time adjusting to her loss. She withdrew from friends who offered to help her and would not discuss Susan's death with anyone other than Tommy. She carried on a silent dialogue with Susan, a behavior that is quite common and not abnormal if it is not carried to extremes. However, when Mrs. Singer tried to blot out her emotional pain by using tranquilizers and by increasing her normal drinking pattern, a neighbor urged her to seek professional help. The doctor persuaded her to join an organization called The Compassionate Friends (see listing at the end of this book). There she met with other parents who had lost children through accidents. She continued to grieve so intensely that she could not adjust to the reality of her loss, even after many months had passed.

Ordinarily, preoccupation with a loss through death comes and goes while a person learns to adjust to it. For Mrs. Singer, whose thoughts were centered around Susan every waking moment, the emotional pain was constant. Her mourning had gone awry.

Mrs. Singer repeated again and again the question so commonly asked by those who suffer loss of a relative or close friend: "Why did this happen?" Some survivors blame God or feel that God is punishing them. Others feel that they have been chosen to play a role of suffering in order to test their faith. Rabbi Harold S. Kushner, who wrote *When Bad Things Happen to Good People,* suggest that misfortunes do not come from God. People feel a sense of relief when they realize that God is not causing their sorrow. Kushner believe that God is a God of justice, not of power, and that people should turn to God for strength and comfort.

While it is normal for people who grieve to suffer from physical problems such as nausea, loss of appetite, or compulsive eating and drinking, these symptoms are short-term. Moodiness and occasional outbursts are common in the first few months, and those who seem strong in the first few weeks often break down at a later period. There is no universal timetable for grieving, but if it extends beyond a few months or a year, counseling should be considered.

Cynthia grieved for her father for two years after he died. She covered her bedroom walls with pictures of him, listened to his favorite records, and stopped visiting with her friends. Although there is nothing wrong with talking to the dead and to experience comfort through dreams, Cynthia had shut herself in a dream world. Her mother expressed concern about her preoccupation with her father's memory, but her grandmother thought it was wonderful that Cynthia was so devoted. Actually, Cynthia was living in a dream where she told herself that her father was devoted to her. He had traveled much of the time when he was alive, and Cynthia had always felt that he neglected her for his new wife. Her mourning was not normal. Although one should not try to forget a family member who has died, it is important to reach out to others and gradually to let go of the loved one.

In their booklet, "When a Brother or Sister Dies," the Compassionate Friends suggest that survivors commit themselves to saying good-bye to the relative who has died, sharing grief with other bereaved siblings, or with caring friends. As a survivor, you should forgive yourself for mean things you have said to the person who died. If you know that it is common to copy some of a brother or sister's interests and habits, and to enjoy living in the past for a while, you may find it easier to go on living. Your grief is unique, and your way of grieving may be unique. Your grief can strengthen you so long as it is not destructive, such as making you do things out of anger because you are hurting so much. You can have fun and enjoy life once more while retaining an emotional bond with the person who died.

Anyone who has lost a beloved person through death knows that special days, such as birthdays, other holidays, and the anniversary of the death can be especially difficult times. Janice Harris Lord, director of Victim Services for Mothers Against Drunk Driving suggests the following for those who have lost someone close to them:

- Ask members of the family with whom you usually celebrate a major holiday to plan in advance. Change some of the traditions, keeping in mind the benefit for those who are hurting most.

- Talk with your family about celebrating Christmas, Passover, and/or other special holidays at the home of a different member of the family. Going away on a vacation to avoid the pain may be worse than facing the pain at home.

- Use the money you would have spent on a gift for the person who died for someone or something that person cared about. Many people find it helpful to become involved in a charity that was important to the person who died.

- Talk about the person who died. Family and friends may hesitate to discuss memories for fear they will upset you. Since the missing person is especially on your mind, you will enjoy the support of friends who also miss him or her.

- You may wish to pay a special tribute to the person who had died. Lighting a special candle, making a special photo

121

album or scrapbook, writing and/or reading a poem, reading a passage from the Bible, Torah, or Koran that was a favorite of the one who died are just a few ways that some families pay special tribute at holiday time.

- Discuss, or think about, several pleasant memories and enjoy them. If you cannot be happy about them, stop.

- At holiday time and at all times, remember that you cannot change the past. Take charge of the present and plan for the future. Do not let the bird of sorrow nest in your hair.

Sources of Further Information

American Association of Suicidology
2459 South Ash
Denver, CO 80222

The Candlelighters Childhood Cancer
    Foundation
2025 Eye Street, N.W., suite 1011
Washington, DC 20006
Local Chapters in Some Areas

The Compassionate Friends
P.O. Box 3696
Oak Brook, IL 60522

Concern for the Dying
250 West 57th Street, Room 831
New York, NY 10107

Forum for Death Education and Counseling
221 Arthur Avenue
Lakewood, OH 44107

Hospice Education Institute
P.O. Box 713
5 Essex Square
Essex, CT 06426

Leukemia Society of America
733 Third Avenue
New York, NY 10017

National Committee on Youth Suicide
  Prevention
666 Fifth Avenue, 13th floor
New York, NY 10103

National Hospice Organization
1901 North Fort Myer Drive, Suite 902
Arlington, VA 22209

Parents of Murdered Children
1739 Bella Vista
Cincinnati, OH 45327

Society for the Right to Die
250 West 57th Street
New York, NY 10107

Youth Suicide National Center
1825 Eye Street N.W., Suite 400
Washington, DC 20006

Suggestions for Further Reading

Deaver, Julie Reece. *Say Goodnight, Gracie.* New York: Harper & Row, 1988. (Fiction)

Hendin, David. *Death As a Fact of Life.* New York: W.W. Norton, 1984.

Hyde, Margaret O., and Elizabeth H. Forsyth. *Suicide: The Hidden Epidemic.* New York: Franklin Watts, 1986.

Jones, Barbara. *Design for Death.* Indianapolis: Bobbs-Merrill, 1967.

Kubler-Ross, Elisabeth. *Death: The Final Stage of Growth.* Englewood Cliffs, N.J.: Prentice-Hall, 1975.

―――. *On Death and Dying.* New York: Macmillan, 1969.

―――. *Questions and Answers on Death and Dying.* New York: Macmillan, 1974.

Kushner, Harold S. *When Bad Things Happen To Good People.* New York: Schocken Books, 1981. New York: Avon, 1983.

Lord, Janice Harris. *No Time for Goodbyes: Coping with Sorrow, Anger, and Injustice After a Tragic Death.* Ventura, Calif.: Pathfinder Press, 1987.

Lukas, Christopher, and Henry M. Seiden. *Silent Grief: Living in the Wake of Suicide.* New York: Charles Scribner's Sons, 1987.

Morgan, Ernest. *Dealing Creatively with Death: A Manual of Death Education and Simple Burial.* Burnsville, N.C.: Celo Press, 1988.

Richter, Elizabeth. *Losing Someone You Love: When a Brother or Sister Dies.* New York: G.P. Putnam, 1986.

Rohr, Janelle, ed. *Death and Dying: Opposing Viewpoints.* St. Paul, Minn.: Greenhaven Press, 1987.

Schneidman, Edwin S., ed. *Death: Current Perspectives*, third edition. New York: Jason Aronson, Inc., 1984.

Segerberg, Osborn. *Living with Death.* New York: E. P. Dutton, 1976.

Index

127